ADVANCED

RSI

INDICATOR

by

Lalit Mohanty

PREFACE

As traders seek to refine their skills and navigate the complexities of financial markets, the Relative Strength Index (RSI) emerges as a versatile and powerful tool for advanced trading strategies. Building upon the foundational principles of RSI, advanced RSI trading delves into nuanced techniques and intricate methodologies that go beyond basic trend identification and signal confirmation.

Advanced RSI trading strategies often involve a sophisticated interplay of RSI with other technical indicators, a deeper understanding of market psychology, and the integration of innovative approaches such as algorithmic trading. This level of expertise allows traders to not only identify potential trend reversals and overbought/oversold conditions but also to extract valuable insights from divergence patterns, implement dynamic risk management, and adapt strategies to various market conditions.

.

Table of Contents:

Chapter 6: Advanced RSI Strategies - Combining Indicators

- 6.1 Integrating RSI with Moving Averages

- 6.2 RSI and Bollinger Bands

- 6.3 Enhancing Predictive Power with Multiple Indicators

Chapter 7: Advanced RSI Strategy - Trend Continuation

- 7.1 Identifying Strong Trends with RSI

- 7.2 Strategies for Riding Trends

- 7.3 Fine-Tuning Entries and Exits

Chapter 8: Advanced RSI Strategy - Fibonacci and RSI

- 8.1 Fibonacci Retracement and Extension Levels

- 8.2 RSI as a Confirmation Tool

- 8.3 Case Studies and Practical Applications

Chapter 9: Advanced RSI Strategy - Quantitative Approaches

- 9.1 Algorithmic Trading with RSI

- 9.2 Statistical Models for RSI Signals

- 9.3 Backtesting and Optimization

Chapter 10: RSI in Different Market Conditions

- 10.1 Adapting RSI Strategies to Bull Markets

- 10.2 Navigating Choppy Markets with RSI

- 10.3 Strategies for Bearish Markets

Chapter 11: Psychology of RSI Trading

CHAPTER 1

INTRODUCTION TO RSI

1.1 Understanding Relative Strength Index

The Relative Strength Index (RSI) is a powerful momentum oscillator that plays a pivotal role in technical analysis, providing traders and investors with insights into the strength and direction of a market's price movements. Developed by J. Welles Wilder in the late 1970s, RSI is widely used to identify overbought and oversold conditions, potential trend reversals, and to gauge the overall momentum within a given security.

1.1.1 Calculation and Formula

At its core, RSI is calculated based on the average gains and losses over a specified time period. The formula involves comparing the average gain to the average loss, resulting in a numerical value that oscillates between 0 and 100. This numerical reading is then plotted on a chart, creating a visual representation of a security's relative strength.

1.1.2 Interpretation of RSI Levels

Understanding RSI levels is crucial for traders. Generally, an RSI reading above 70 is considered overbought, indicating that the security may be due for a pullback. Conversely, an RSI reading below 30 is considered oversold, suggesting that the security may be undervalued and due for a potential rebound. Traders use these levels to make informed decisions about buying or selling assets.

1.1.3 Identifying Overbought and Oversold Conditions

Overbought and oversold conditions are key concepts when using RSI. Overbought conditions suggest that a security may be overvalued, potentially signaling an impending correction. On the other hand, oversold conditions indicate that a security may be undervalued, suggesting a possible buying opportunity. Recognizing these conditions helps traders anticipate market reversals and make informed decisions.

1.2 Importance of RSI in Technical Analysis

RSI holds a central position in technical analysis due to its ability to provide timely and actionable information. It offers insights into a security's internal strength, helping traders and investors make informed decisions. The importance of RSI in technical analysis can be summarized as follows:

1.2.1 Trend Reversals

RSI is particularly effective in identifying potential trend reversals. When RSI diverges from the price trend, it can signal a weakening trend and the possibility of a reversal. Traders often look for these divergences as early indications of a change in market direction.

1.2.2 Confirmation of Trends

RSI is frequently used to confirm the strength of existing trends. A rising RSI in an uptrend indicates strong buying momentum, while a falling RSI in a downtrend suggests robust selling pressure. This confirmation allows traders to align their positions with the prevailing trend.

1.2.3 Timing Entries and Exits

By pinpointing overbought and oversold conditions, RSI aids in timing entry and exit points. Traders can use RSI to enter a trade when a security is oversold and exit when it becomes overbought. This disciplined approach enhances the probability of successful trades.

1.3 Historical Perspective

The development of RSI by J. Welles Wilder marked a significant milestone in technical analysis. Introduced in Wilder's book "New Concepts in Technical Trading Systems" in 1978, RSI quickly gained popularity among traders for its ability to provide valuable insights into market dynamics.

Over the years, RSI has evolved into a versatile tool, finding applications across various financial markets, including stocks, forex, commodities, and cryptocurrencies. Its adaptability to different time frames and trading styles has contributed to its enduring relevance in the ever-changing landscape of financial markets.

As we delve deeper into this guide, we will explore how traders can harness the power of RSI through basic and advanced strategies, unlocking its full potential for effective decision-making in the dynamic world of trading.

CHAPTER 2

BASICS OF RSI

2.1 Calculation and Formula

Understanding the calculation and formula of the Relative Strength Index (RSI) is fundamental for any trader looking to incorporate this oscillator into their technical analysis toolkit. The RSI calculation involves several steps:

2.1.1 Average Gain and Loss Calculation

1. **Calculate Daily Price Changes:**

    - For each trading day, calculate the price change by subtracting the previous day's close from the current day's close.

2. **Separate Gains and Losses:**

    - Separate the price changes into gains (positive changes) and losses (negative changes). If the price change is zero or negative, consider it a loss.

3. **Calculate Average Gain and Loss:**

- Calculate the average gain and average loss over a specified period, often 14 days. The average gain is the sum of gains over the chosen period divided by the number of periods, and the average loss is the sum of losses divided by the number of periods.

2.1.2 Relative Strength Calculation

4. **Calculate Relative Strength (RS):**

- Divide the average gain by the average loss to obtain the relative strength (RS) value.

2.1.3 RSI Calculation

5. **Calculate RSI:**

- Use the following formula to calculate RSI: 100-100/(1+RS)

The result is a numerical value that ranges between 0 and 100, representing the strength and magnitude of recent price changes.

2.2 Interpretation of RSI Levels

Interpreting RSI levels is crucial for making informed trading decisions. RSI values are typically displayed on a scale from 0 to 100, with key levels that traders commonly reference:

2.2.1 Overbought Conditions (RSI above 70)

- **Cautionary Signal:** RSI readings above 70 suggest that the asset may be overbought.

- **Potential Reversal:** Traders often interpret overbought conditions as a potential signal for an impending price correction or trend reversal.

- **Considered High Risk:** Buying into an asset when RSI is in overbought territory carries a higher risk, and traders may exercise caution.

2.2.2 Oversold Conditions (RSI below 30)

- **Cautionary Signal:** RSI readings below 30 indicate that the asset may be oversold.

- **Potential Reversal:** Oversold conditions may suggest a possible buying opportunity, as the price may be due for a rebound.

- **Considered High Reward:** Entering a trade when RSI is oversold carries the potential for high rewards if the anticipated rebound occurs.

2.2.3 Neutral Zone (RSI between 30 and 70)

- **Stable Conditions:** RSI readings between 30 and 70 are considered neutral, indicating a relatively stable market.

- **Trend Confirmation:** During trending markets, RSI within this range may confirm the strength and sustainability of the trend.

- **Watch for Changes:** Traders closely monitor RSI within the neutral zone for potential shifts in market sentiment.

2.3 Identifying Overbought and Oversold Conditions

Identifying overbought and oversold conditions using RSI involves more than just looking at numerical levels. Traders often use the following guidelines:

2.3.1 Overbought Conditions

- **Divergence with Price:** If the price is making new highs, but RSI fails to follow suit and starts trending downward, it could signal weakening momentum and an overbought condition.

- **Sharp Price Increase:** A rapid and sharp increase in price over a short period can lead to an overbought condition, especially if the pace of the ascent is not sustainable.

2.3.2 Oversold Conditions

- **Divergence with Price:** When the price is making new lows, but RSI fails to confirm these lows and starts moving upward, it may indicate a potential bullish reversal and an oversold condition.

- **Sharp Price Decline:** A steep and rapid decline in price over a short period can lead to an oversold condition, suggesting that the selling pressure may be excessive.

Understanding the basics of RSI, its calculation, interpretation of levels, and the identification of overbought and oversold conditions lays a solid foundation for applying this powerful tool in trading. As we progress through this guide, we will explore various strategies that leverage these basic concepts for effective decision-making in diverse market scenarios.

CHAPTER 3

BASIC RSI STRATEGY - TREND REVERSALS

3.1 Recognizing Trend Reversals with RSI

One of the primary applications of the Relative Strength Index (RSI) is in identifying potential trend reversals. Recognizing when a prevailing trend may be losing strength or reversing is crucial for traders seeking to capitalize on shifts in market direction. Several key signals and patterns can assist in recognizing trend reversals with RSI:

3.1.1 RSI Divergence

- **Regular Divergence:** Occurs when the price makes a new high or low, but RSI fails to confirm the same high or low. Regular divergence can signal weakening momentum and hint at a possible trend reversal.

- **Hidden Divergence:** Involves the price making a new high or low, while RSI confirms the same high or low. Hidden divergence can indicate strong momentum and potential continuation of the trend.

3.1.2 RSI Trendline Breaks

- **Trendline on RSI:** Drawing trendlines on RSI can help identify potential trend reversals. A break in the trendline on RSI may precede a reversal in the price trend.

3.1.3 RSI Extreme Readings

- **Overbought and Oversold Conditions:** RSI reaching extreme levels, such as above 70 (overbought) or below 30 (oversold), can signal that a trend might be losing steam and a reversal could be imminent.

3.2 Entry and Exit Points

Having recognized a potential trend reversal with RSI, traders can then plan entry and exit points to capitalize on the changing market dynamics:

3.2.1 Entry Points

- **Wait for Confirmation:** Enter a trade when there is confirmation from both RSI signals and the price action. This confirmation helps reduce false signals.

- **Divergence Confirmation:** Confirm RSI divergence with other technical indicators or chart patterns before making an entry decision.

- **Candlestick Patterns:** Look for reversal candlestick patterns on price charts, such as engulfing patterns or doji candles, to enhance the reliability of entry points.

3.2.2 Exit Points

- **Take Profits Gradually:** Consider scaling out of a position gradually as the trend reversal progresses. This allows traders to lock in profits at various levels.

- **RSI Crossing Back:** Exit the trade if RSI starts to move back into overbought or oversold territory opposite to the expected reversal.

- **Price Confirmation:** Monitor the price action for signs of a trend resumption or a strong countertrend move. Exiting a trade based on price action can provide additional confirmation.

3.3 Risk Management Techniques

Effectively managing risk is paramount in any trading strategy, and the basic RSI strategy for trend reversals is no exception. Implementing sound risk management techniques can help protect capital and enhance the overall success of the strategy:

3.3.1 Set Stop-Loss Orders

- **Based on Volatility:** Adjust stop-loss levels based on the volatility of the asset. More volatile assets may require wider stops to account for price fluctuations.

- **Technical Levels:** Place stop-loss orders below or above key technical levels, such as support or resistance, to minimize the impact of false signals.

3.3.2 Position Sizing

- **Determine Position Size:** Calculate the position size based on the level of risk tolerance and the distance to the stop-loss level. This ensures that each trade carries a consistent risk percentage.

- **Diversify Positions:** Avoid concentrating too much capital on a single trade. Diversifying positions across different assets helps spread risk.

3.3.3 Risk-Reward Ratio

- **Favorable Risk-Reward Ratio:** Ensure that the potential reward justifies the risk taken in each trade. A common guideline is to aim for a risk-reward ratio of at least 1:2.

- **Adapt to Market Conditions:** Adjust risk-reward ratios based on market conditions and the overall trend. In trending markets, traders may consider more aggressive risk-reward ratios.

The basic RSI strategy for trend reversals provides a systematic approach to identifying and capitalizing on shifts in market direction. By recognizing RSI signals, carefully planning entry and exit points, and implementing effective risk management, traders can enhance their ability to navigate the dynamic landscape of trend reversals with confidence. As we progress through this guide, more advanced RSI strategies will be explored, building upon these foundational principles.

CHAPTER 4

BASIC RSI STRATEGY – DIVERGENCE

4.1 Understanding Divergence

Divergence is a key concept in technical analysis and a central element of many trading strategies, including those involving the Relative Strength Index (RSI). Divergence occurs when there is a disagreement between the price action of an asset and an accompanying technical indicator, such as RSI. Understanding divergence is crucial for traders as it can signal potential changes in trend direction and provide insights into the underlying strength or weakness of a market.

4.1.1 Regular Divergence

- **Bullish Regular Divergence:** Occurs when the price forms lower lows while the RSI forms higher lows. This suggests that the momentum behind the price decline is weakening, and a bullish reversal might be on the horizon.

- **Bearish Regular Divergence:** Happens when the price forms higher highs while the RSI forms lower highs. This indicates that the upward momentum is waning, and a bearish reversal may be imminent.

4.1.2 Hidden Divergence

- **Bullish Hidden Divergence:** Takes place when the price forms higher lows while the RSI forms lower lows. This suggests that despite a pullback in price, the underlying bullish momentum remains strong.

- **Bearish Hidden Divergence:** Occurs when the price forms lower highs while the RSI forms higher highs. This signals that, despite a price rally, the underlying bearish momentum persists.

4.2 Spotting Bullish and Bearish Divergence

Recognizing divergence involves keen observation of both price action and RSI readings. Traders can use various methods to spot bullish and bearish divergence:

4.2.1 Visual Inspection

- **Comparing Peaks and Troughs:** Visually inspect the price chart alongside the RSI chart, comparing the peaks and troughs. Look for instances where the price and RSI are moving in opposite directions.

- **Pattern Recognition:** Bullish and bearish divergence often occurs in recognizable patterns, such as double tops or bottoms. Identifying these patterns can enhance divergence analysis.

4.2.2 RSI Trendline

- **Drawing RSI Trendlines:** Draw trendlines on the RSI chart connecting the highs or lows. A break in these trendlines can be a strong signal of divergence.

4.2.3 Indicator Confirmation

- **Using Other Indicators:** Confirm RSI divergence signals with other technical indicators, such as moving averages or trend indicators. Additional confirmation strengthens the validity of divergence signals.

4.3 Trading Strategies based on Divergence Signals

Once divergence is identified, traders can implement various strategies to capitalize on potential trend reversals:

4.3.1 Entry Points

- **Confirmation from Price Action:** Wait for confirmation from the price action to validate the divergence signal before entering a trade.

- **Combining with Support/Resistance:** Use divergence signals in conjunction with key support or resistance levels for more robust entry points.

4.3.2 Exit Points

- **RSI Crossing Back:** Consider exiting the trade when RSI starts to move back in the opposite direction, indicating a potential change in momentum.

- **Price Confirmation:** Monitor the price for confirmation of a reversal or a strong countertrend move before exiting the trade.

4.3.3 Risk Management

- **Setting Stop-Loss Orders:** Place stop-loss orders to manage risk, taking into account the distance to key technical levels and the overall risk tolerance.

- **Scaling Positions:** Scale out of a position gradually as the divergence signal unfolds, allowing for partial profit-taking at various levels.

Divergence is a potent tool for traders using RSI, providing valuable insights into potential trend reversals. By understanding the nuances of regular and hidden divergence, spotting these signals, and implementing effective entry, exit, and risk management strategies, traders can enhance their ability to navigate markets with greater precision. In the subsequent chapters, we will delve into more advanced RSI strategies, building upon the foundational principles of divergence discussed here.

CHAPTER 5

BASIC RSI STRATEGY - SUPPORT AND RESISTANCE

5.1 Utilizing RSI in Conjunction with Support and Resistance

Support and resistance are fundamental concepts in technical analysis, representing key levels at which an asset's price has historically had difficulty moving beyond (resistance) or falling below (support). When combined with the Relative Strength Index (RSI), these levels offer valuable insights into potential trend reversals and trend continuation.

5.1.1 Identifying Support and Resistance

- **Historical Price Levels:** Identify historical price levels where the asset has previously faced resistance or found support. These can be identified through peaks and troughs on a price chart.

- **Psychological Levels:** Consider psychological levels, such as round numbers or historical highs/lows, as potential support or resistance.

5.1.2 RSI at Support and Resistance

- **Oversold at Support:** When the price approaches a support level and RSI is in oversold territory (below 30), it may signal that selling pressure is exhausted, and a potential rebound could occur.

- **Overbought at Resistance:** Conversely, when the price approaches a resistance level and RSI is in overbought territory (above 70), it may indicate that buying momentum is waning, and a reversal could be on the horizon.

5.2 Confirmation Signals

Utilizing RSI in conjunction with support and resistance levels involves seeking confirmation signals to enhance the reliability of trading decisions:

5.2.1 Candlestick Patterns

- **Reversal Candlesticks:** Look for reversal candlestick patterns, such as doji, engulfing, or hammer patterns, at key support or resistance levels. These patterns can confirm potential reversals.

5.2.2 Trendline Analysis

- **Trendline Breaks:** Draw trendlines on both the price chart and RSI chart. A break in the trendline on both charts can serve as a strong confirmation signal.

5.2.3 Volume Analysis

- **Volume Surge:** Analyze trading volume when the price approaches support or resistance. A surge in volume accompanying a bounce or reversal can strengthen the likelihood of a valid signal.

5.3 Case Studies

Understanding how to apply RSI in conjunction with support and resistance is best illustrated through practical examples. Let's explore two case studies:

5.3.1 Case Study 1: Support Bounce

- **Scenario:** Price approaches a historical support level, and RSI is in oversold territory.

- **Confirmation Signal:** A bullish reversal candlestick pattern forms at the support level, accompanied by a notable increase in volume.

- **Trade Execution:** A trader enters a long position, anticipating a bounce off the support level.

5.3.2 Case Study 2: Resistance Reversal

- **Scenario:** Price approaches a historical resistance level, and RSI is in overbought territory.

- **Confirmation Signal:** A bearish reversal candlestick pattern forms at the resistance level, and there is a decline in trading volume.

- **Trade Execution:** A trader enters a short position, anticipating a reversal from the resistance level.

These case studies illustrate how combining RSI with support and resistance levels, along with confirmation signals, can provide a comprehensive framework for making informed trading decisions.

In summary, utilizing RSI in conjunction with support and resistance levels enhances a trader's ability to identify potential trend reversals and trend continuation. By seeking confirmation signals and studying real-world case studies, traders can gain practical insights into applying this strategy effectively. As we progress through this guide, we will delve into more advanced RSI strategies, building upon the foundational principles discussed here.

CHAPTER 6

ADVANCED RSI STRATEGIES - COMBINING INDICATORS

6.1 Integrating RSI with Moving Averages

Combining the Relative Strength Index (RSI) with moving averages is a powerful approach that leverages the strengths of both indicators to provide enhanced signals for traders. This integration allows for a more comprehensive analysis of price trends, momentum, and potential reversals.

6.1.1 Moving Average Crossovers

- **Golden Cross:** Combining a long-term moving average (e.g., 50-day) with RSI, a golden cross occurs when the price moves above the moving average, and RSI confirms the upward momentum, signaling a potential bullish trend.

- **Death Cross:** Conversely, a death cross occurs when the price moves below the moving average, and RSI confirms the downward momentum, indicating a potential bearish trend.

6.1.2 Trend Confirmation

- **Trend Alignment:** Confirm the prevailing trend by observing the alignment of RSI with the moving average. In an uptrend, RSI should generally stay above 50, while in a downtrend, it should stay below 50.

- **Divergence Confirmation:** Use moving averages to confirm RSI divergence signals, providing additional validation for potential trend reversals.

6.2 RSI and Bollinger Bands

Integrating RSI with Bollinger Bands, which consist of a middle band (usually a 20-day simple moving average) and two standard deviation bands, offers insights into volatility, overbought, and oversold conditions.

6.2.1 Bollinger Bands Squeeze

- **Volatility Contraction:** When Bollinger Bands contract, indicating low volatility, and RSI is trading in overbought or oversold territory, it may signal an impending price breakout.

- **Confirmation with RSI:** RSI readings above 70 in conjunction with the upper Bollinger Band can indicate overbought conditions, potentially signaling an upcoming reversal. Conversely, RSI readings below 30 with the lower Bollinger Band may suggest oversold conditions.

6.2.2 Riding the Bands

- **Trend Continuation:** During strong trends, prices may ride the upper or lower Bollinger Band. Confirm these trends using RSI. In an uptrend, RSI tends to stay above 50, and in a downtrend, RSI remains below 50.

- **Divergence Confirmation:** If price reaches a new high or low outside the Bollinger Bands, and RSI does not confirm the same, it may signal a potential reversal.

6.3 Enhancing Predictive Power with Multiple Indicators

The use of multiple indicators, including RSI, in tandem enhances the predictive power of trading strategies. Each indicator provides unique insights, and their convergence can strengthen signals.

6.3.1 Confirmatory Signals

- **RSI and MACD:** Combining RSI with the Moving Average Convergence Divergence (MACD) can offer confirmatory signals. For instance, an RSI divergence accompanied by a MACD crossover strengthens the potential reversal signal.

- **Stochastic and RSI:** Integrating the Stochastic Oscillator with RSI can provide additional confirmation. For example, if RSI indicates overbought conditions and the Stochastic confirms with a bearish crossover, it strengthens the sell signal.

6.3.2 Comprehensive Analysis

- **Trend Confirmation:** Use trend indicators like moving averages alongside RSI for trend confirmation. If RSI signals a reversal, but the moving average remains aligned with the prevailing trend, exercise caution.

- **Volume Analysis:** Consider incorporating volume indicators with RSI. An RSI divergence accompanied by a surge in volume can enhance the reliability of the signal.

6.3.3 Dynamic Risk Management

- **Multi-Indicator Risk Assessment:** Analyze risk across multiple indicators. If various indicators provide conflicting signals, consider reducing position size or avoiding the trade altogether.

- **Adaptability:** Adjust risk management strategies based on the collective insights from multiple indicators. A comprehensive approach allows for more dynamic risk management.

By integrating RSI with moving averages, Bollinger Bands, and other indicators, traders can build more robust and versatile strategies. The synergy of these indicators provides a more nuanced understanding of market conditions, helping traders make informed decisions with enhanced predictive power. As we progress through this guide, we will explore additional advanced RSI strategies, further refining our approach to trading.

CHAPTER 7

ADVANCED RSI STRATEGY - TREND CONTINUATION

7.1 Identifying Strong Trends with RSI

The ability to identify and capitalize on strong trends is a key element of successful trading. The Relative Strength Index (RSI) can be a valuable tool in identifying and confirming the strength of trends, providing insights for trend continuation strategies.

7.1.1 Trend Confirmation with RSI

- **RSI Trend Confirmation:** In a strong uptrend, RSI tends to stay above the 50 level, reflecting consistent buying pressure. Conversely, in a downtrend, RSI often remains below 50, indicating sustained selling momentum.

- **Divergence Analysis:** Look for divergence between RSI and price trends. If RSI confirms the trend by making new highs in an uptrend or new lows in a downtrend, it supports the continuation of the trend.

7.2 Strategies for Riding Trends

Once a strong trend is identified, traders can employ specific strategies to ride the trend and maximize profit potential.

7.2.1 RSI Trendline Breaks

- **Entering on Trendline Breaks:** Draw trendlines on RSI corresponding to the prevailing trend. Enter a trade when RSI breaks above the trendline in an uptrend or below the trendline in a downtrend, confirming the strength of the trend.

- **Risk Management:** Set stop-loss orders based on the trendline break, ensuring that the trade is exited if the trend loses its strength.

7.2.2 RSI Pullback Entry

- **Wait for RSI Pullbacks:** In a strong trend, RSI may temporarily dip below 50 during minor pullbacks. Enter a trade when RSI bounces back above 50, indicating a potential resumption of the trend.

- **Confirm with Price Action:** Confirm RSI signals with price action, ensuring that the asset's price aligns with the anticipated trend continuation.

7.3 Fine-Tuning Entries and Exits

Fine-tuning entries and exits is crucial for maximizing profitability and minimizing risk when riding trends with RSI.

7.3.1 Fine-Tuning Entry Points

- **Using Support and Resistance:** Identify key support and resistance levels in the direction of the trend. Enter the trade when RSI aligns with these levels, providing additional confirmation.

- **Volume Confirmation:** Confirm trend continuation entries with an increase in trading volume. A surge in volume suggests strong market participation, supporting the validity of the trend.

7.3.2 Fine-Tuning Exit Points

- **Monitoring RSI Levels:** Continuously monitor RSI levels. In a strong uptrend, consider exiting when RSI reaches overbought territory (above 70). In a downtrend, exit when RSI reaches oversold territory (below 30).

- **Price Confirmation:** Use price action to confirm potential trend reversals. Exit the trade if there are signs of a significant price reversal against the trend.

7.3.3 Trailing Stop-Loss

- **Implementing Trailing Stops:** Trail stop-loss orders behind the trend to lock in profits as the trend progresses. Adjust the trailing stop as the price moves in the desired direction.

- **Dynamic Adjustments:** Dynamically adjust the trailing stop based on the volatility of the asset. Wider trailing stops may be suitable for more volatile assets.

By effectively identifying strong trends with RSI, implementing trend continuation strategies, and fine-tuning entries and exits, traders can optimize their approach to riding trends. This advanced RSI strategy allows for more precise decision-making, enhancing the potential for profitable trades. As we progress through this guide, we will explore additional advanced RSI strategies, building upon the foundational principles discussed here.

CHAPTER 8

ADVANCED RSI STRATEGY - FIBONACCI AND RSI

8.1 Fibonacci Retracement and Extension Levels

Integrating Fibonacci retracement and extension levels with the Relative Strength Index (RSI) adds a sophisticated layer to technical analysis. Fibonacci levels are based on the mathematical relationships derived from the Fibonacci sequence and are commonly used to identify potential reversal or extension points in price trends.

8.1.1 Fibonacci Retracement Levels

- **Identifying Retracement Levels:** Apply Fibonacci retracement levels to significant price swings. The key levels include 38.2%, 50%, and 61.8%. These levels help identify potential retracement areas during a trend.

- **RSI Confirmation:** Confirm retracement levels with RSI. Look for oversold conditions (RSI below 30) at or near Fibonacci support levels during an uptrend, or overbought conditions (RSI above 70) at or near Fibonacci resistance levels during a downtrend.

8.1.2 Fibonacci Extension Levels

- **Spotting Extension Opportunities:** Apply Fibonacci extension levels to identify potential price extension areas. Common extension levels include 127.2%, 161.8%, and 261.8%. These levels indicate potential targets for trend continuation.

- **RSI as a Leading Indicator:** Use RSI as a leading indicator to spot potential reversals or extensions before price reaches the Fibonacci levels. Divergence between RSI and price at Fibonacci extension points can strengthen signals.

8.2 RSI as a Confirmation Tool

RSI serves as an effective confirmation tool when combined with Fibonacci levels, enhancing the reliability of signals and providing a more comprehensive view of market conditions.

8.2.1 Divergence Confirmation

- **Divergence at Fibonacci Levels:** Confirm potential reversals or extensions identified by Fibonacci levels with RSI divergence. If RSI diverges from the price action at a Fibonacci level, it strengthens the signal.

- **Hidden Divergence Confirmation:** In the context of Fibonacci extensions, hidden divergence on RSI can confirm the strength of an ongoing trend, supporting the idea of a potential extension beyond the standard Fibonacci levels.

8.2.2 RSI Trendline Breaks

- **Trendline Breaks in Conjunction with Fib Levels:** Draw trendlines on RSI corresponding to the prevailing trend. Enter a trade when RSI breaks above or below the trendline near a Fibonacci level, confirming the strength of the trend or potential reversal.

- **Dynamic Confirmation:** As the trend progresses, use RSI trendline breaks near Fibonacci levels as dynamic confirmation for adjusting stop-loss levels or scaling into/out of positions.

8.3 Case Studies and Practical Applications

To illustrate the practical application of the advanced strategy combining Fibonacci and RSI, let's explore two case studies:

8.3.1 Case Study 1: Fibonacci Retracement and RSI

- **Scenario:** The price is in an uptrend and retraces to the 50% Fibonacci level.

- **RSI Confirmation:** RSI shows oversold conditions (below 30) near the 50% retracement level.

- **Trade Execution:** A trader enters a long position, anticipating a bounce based on the confluence of RSI oversold conditions and the Fibonacci retracement level.

8.3.2 Case Study 2: Fibonacci Extension and RSI

- **Scenario:** The price is in a strong uptrend, and a potential extension is identified using Fibonacci extension levels.

- **RSI Confirmation:** RSI shows hidden divergence, making higher lows while the price makes higher highs, confirming the strength of the uptrend.

- **Trade Execution:** A trader enters a long position, expecting the trend to continue based on the confluence of hidden divergence and the Fibonacci extension levels.

These case studies demonstrate how combining Fibonacci levels with RSI can provide a robust framework for making advanced trading decisions. By leveraging RSI as a confirmation tool, traders can enhance the precision of their entries and exits, increasing the likelihood of successful trades.

As we delve deeper into advanced RSI strategies, it becomes evident that the synergy between technical tools can significantly elevate the effectiveness of trading approaches. Understanding the intricacies of combining Fibonacci and RSI empowers traders to navigate complex market scenarios with increased confidence and precision.

CHAPTER 9

ADVANCED RSI STRATEGY – QUANTITATIVE APPROACHES

9.1 Algorithmic Trading with RSI

Algorithmic trading involves the use of computer programs to execute trading strategies. When applied to RSI, algorithmic trading can automate the process of identifying signals, entering and exiting trades, and managing risk. This approach leverages the speed and efficiency of computers to execute trades based on predefined rules.

9.1.1 Signal Generation Algorithms

- **RSI Thresholds:** Develop algorithms that trigger trades based on specific RSI thresholds. For example, buying when RSI crosses above 70 and selling when it drops below 30.

- **Divergence Detection:** Incorporate algorithms that identify regular or hidden divergence patterns on RSI, automatically generating buy or sell signals.

9.1.2 Risk Management Algorithms

- **Dynamic Position Sizing:** Implement algorithms that dynamically adjust position sizes based on factors like volatility or account equity. This helps optimize risk management in varying market conditions.

- **Trailing Stops:** Utilize algorithms to automate trailing stop-loss orders, adjusting them as the trade progresses and RSI conditions evolve.

9.2 Statistical Models for RSI Signals

Statistical models provide a quantitative framework for analyzing RSI signals, allowing traders to make decisions based on historical data patterns. These models can range from simple statistical analyses to more complex machine learning approaches.

9.2.1 Regression Analysis

- **Historical Correlations:** Use regression analysis to identify historical correlations between RSI levels and subsequent price movements. This helps quantify the relationship between RSI signals and price trends.

- **Coefficient Significance:** Assess the significance of coefficients to prioritize the most relevant RSI parameters for generating signals.

9.2.2 Machine Learning Models

- **Training Data:** Feed historical market data into machine learning models to train them on recognizing patterns associated with successful RSI signals.

- **Feature Importance:** Identify important features, such as specific RSI timeframes or market conditions, through feature importance analysis to refine model inputs.

9.3 Backtesting and Optimization

Backtesting involves applying a trading strategy to historical market data to assess its performance. Optimization aims to fine-tune the strategy parameters for better historical performance, keeping in mind the risk of overfitting.

9.3.1 Backtesting Strategies

- **Historical Data Simulation:** Use historical market data to simulate trades based on the algorithmic or statistical strategy.

- **Performance Metrics:** Evaluate the strategy's performance using metrics such as profitability, risk-adjusted returns, and maximum drawdown.

9.3.2 Optimization Techniques

- **Parameter Tuning:** Adjust strategy parameters based on backtesting results to optimize performance. This may involve fine-tuning RSI thresholds, lookback periods, or other variables.

- **Out-of-Sample Testing:** Validate the optimized strategy on out-of-sample data to ensure robustness and avoid overfitting to specific historical patterns.

Conclusion

Quantitative approaches to RSI strategies, whether through algorithmic trading, statistical models, or optimization techniques, offer a systematic and data-driven way to navigate financial markets. By leveraging the power of quantitative analysis, traders can enhance their decision-making processes, manage risk more effectively, and potentially uncover new insights into the dynamics of RSI signals.

As with any advanced strategy, it is crucial for traders to exercise caution, thoroughly test their models, and adapt to changing market conditions. The intersection of quantitative approaches and RSI strategies represents an exciting frontier in the ever-evolving landscape of algorithmic trading and quantitative finance.

CHAPTER 10

RSI IN DIFFERENT MARKET CONDITIONS

The Relative Strength Index (RSI) is a versatile tool that traders can adapt to various market conditions. Understanding how to tailor RSI strategies to different market environments enhances a trader's ability to make informed decisions across a range of scenarios.

10.1 Adapting RSI Strategies to Bull Markets

Bull markets are characterized by rising prices and optimistic sentiment. Adapting RSI strategies to thrive in bull markets involves identifying trends and momentum continuation.

10.1.1 Trend Confirmation

- **Trend Riding:** In bull markets, RSI tends to remain in overbought territory for extended periods. Instead of using overbought conditions as reversal signals, consider them as confirmation of strong upward momentum.

- **Hidden Divergence:** Look for hidden bullish divergence, where RSI makes higher lows while the price makes lower lows. This signals strong upward momentum despite temporary pullbacks.

10.1.2 Volatility Adjustments

- **Wider Bands:** Incorporate wider Bollinger Bands or adjust RSI thresholds to account for increased volatility. Bull markets often experience higher volatility, and broader parameters may prevent premature exits.

- **Dynamic Risk Management:** Implement dynamic risk management techniques, such as trailing stops, to capture potential extended trends while protecting profits during pullbacks.

10.2 Navigating Choppy Markets with RSI

Choppy markets, characterized by erratic price movements and indecision among market participants, pose challenges for trend-following strategies. Adapting RSI in choppy markets involves recognizing range-bound conditions.

10.2.1 Range Identification

- **RSI Range:** Identify a narrower RSI range that corresponds to the choppiness in the market. For example, use RSI levels between 40 and 60 to signal potential reversals in a range-bound market.

- **Bollinger Band Contraction:** Look for periods of Bollinger Band contraction, indicating lower volatility and potential range-bound conditions.

10.2.2 Mean Reversion Strategies

- **Overbought/Oversold Reversals:** In choppy markets, consider using RSI to identify overbought or oversold conditions for mean reversion trades. Trade against extreme RSI readings expecting a return to the mean.

- **Divergence Signals:** Leverage regular divergence signals to identify potential reversal points within the range. These divergences may indicate shifts in market sentiment.

10.3 Strategies for Bearish Markets

Bear markets are characterized by declining prices and increased pessimism among investors. Adapting RSI strategies to bearish markets involves capitalizing on downtrends and managing risk effectively.

10.3.1 Trend Following in Downtrends

- **Below 50 Threshold:** In bear markets, RSI often stays below 50, signaling persistent selling pressure. Use RSI below 50 as confirmation of the prevailing downtrend.

- **Trendline Breaks:** Identify trendline breaks on RSI to signal potential acceleration in the downtrend. Enter trades when RSI breaks below a trendline in a bearish market.

10.3.2 Safe Haven Assets

- **Utilizing Safe Havens:** In bearish markets, consider incorporating RSI strategies on safe-haven assets like gold or government bonds. These assets may exhibit different dynamics than traditional equities.

- **Flight to Quality Signals:** Monitor RSI signals on assets known for their stability during market downturns. RSI levels on these assets may provide early indications of a broader market downturn.

Conclusion

Adapting RSI strategies to different market conditions requires a nuanced understanding of the unique dynamics at play during bull markets, choppy markets, and bear markets. Traders should be flexible in their approach, recognizing that no single strategy fits all scenarios. By tailoring RSI strategies to specific market conditions, traders can enhance their ability to navigate the complexities of the financial markets and make more informed decisions. As we conclude this guide, remember that successful trading often involves a blend of technical analysis, risk management, and adaptability to evolving market conditions.

CHAPTER 11

PSYCHOLOGY OF RSI TRADING

Trading with the Relative Strength Index (RSI) not only involves technical analysis but also requires a deep understanding of the psychological aspects of trading. Mastering the psychology of RSI trading is essential for maintaining emotional discipline, managing fear and greed, and developing a structured trading plan.

11.1 Emotional Discipline and Patience

11.1.1 Discipline in Following RSI Signals

- **Sticking to the Plan:** Emotional discipline involves adhering to your predefined RSI trading plan. Trust in the signals generated by RSI and avoid making impulsive decisions based on emotions.

- **Avoiding Impatience:** RSI signals may not always result in immediate market movements. Patience is crucial, as trends may take time to develop. Avoid impulsive actions based on short-term fluctuations.

11.1.2 Rational Decision-Making

- **Objective Analysis:** Embrace a rational and objective mindset when interpreting RSI signals. Avoid being swayed by emotions, rumors, or short-term market noise.

- **Learning from Mistakes:** If a trade doesn't go as planned, focus on learning from the experience rather than dwelling on the outcome. Emotional discipline involves acknowledging mistakes and using them as opportunities for improvement.

11.2 Managing Fear and Greed

11.2.1 Fear of Missing Out (FOMO)

- **Disciplined Entry and Exit:** Fear of missing out can lead to impulsive trades. Stick to your trading plan, enter positions based on well-defined RSI signals, and avoid chasing the market.

- **Risk Management:** Implement effective risk management strategies to mitigate the fear of losses. Set stop-loss orders based on your risk tolerance and let the market play out according to your plan.

11.2.2 Greed and Overtrading

- **Avoiding Overtrading:** Greed can tempt traders to overtrade or deviate from their strategy. Set realistic profit targets and recognize when it's time to step back and assess market conditions without getting caught in excessive trading.

- **Taking Profits:** Greed can also prevent traders from taking profits at appropriate levels. Set clear profit-taking targets based on RSI signals and stick to them to avoid missing out on gains.

11.3 Developing a Trading Plan

11.3.1 Clearly Defined Rules

- **Entry and Exit Criteria:** Clearly define the criteria for entering and exiting trades based on RSI signals. Having a set of rules helps remove emotions from decision-making.

- **Risk-Reward Ratios:** Establish risk-reward ratios for each trade. Determine the amount of capital at risk in relation to the potential profit. This ensures a systematic approach to risk management.

11.3.2 Backtesting and Evaluation

- **Backtesting Strategies:** Before implementing a trading plan, backtest it using historical data to assess its performance. This helps in refining and optimizing the strategy.

- **Regular Evaluation:** Markets evolve, and so should your trading plan. Regularly evaluate the effectiveness of your strategy, considering changes in market conditions or your risk tolerance.

11.3.3 Journaling and Reflection

- **Trade Journal:** Maintain a detailed trade journal to record each trade, including the rationale, entry and exit points, and emotions felt during the trade. This helps in identifying patterns, strengths, and areas for improvement.

- **Continuous Learning:** Treat trading as a continuous learning process. Reflect on both successful and unsuccessful trades, extracting lessons that contribute to your evolving trading strategy.

Conclusion

Mastering the psychology of RSI trading is a journey that involves cultivating emotional discipline, managing fear and greed, and developing a robust trading plan. Recognizing the psychological challenges inherent in trading and actively working to overcome them is integral to becoming a successful RSI trader. As you embark on your trading journey, remember that psychological resilience is as important as technical proficiency, and a well-balanced approach will contribute to long-term success in the dynamic world of financial markets.

CHAPTER 12

RSI STRATEGY FOR FOREX MARKETS

The Foreign Exchange (Forex) market, known for its dynamic nature, provides ample opportunities for traders. Applying the Relative Strength Index (RSI) to the Forex market requires a nuanced approach, considering the unique characteristics of currency trading.

12.1 Currency Trading and RSI

12.1.1 Forex Market Dynamics

- **24-Hour Market:** The Forex market operates 24 hours a day, five days a week, allowing for continuous price movements and various trading sessions.

- **High Liquidity:** Currency pairs are highly liquid, facilitating easy entry and exit for traders.

12.1.2 Sensitivity to Economic Factors

- **Fundamental Influences:** Economic indicators, interest rates, and geopolitical events significantly impact currency prices.

- **Intermarket Relationships:** Currency pairs often react to global economic trends and relationships with commodities, equities, and other financial markets.

12.2 Applying RSI to Major and Minor Pairs

12.2.1 Major Currency Pairs

- **EUR/USD, USD/JPY, GBP/USD, USD/CHF:** Apply traditional RSI strategies, focusing on trend reversals, overbought/oversold conditions, and divergence signals.

- **Long-Term Trends:** Consider using higher RSI periods (e.g., 14 or 21) for assessing longer-term trends in major pairs.

12.2.2 Minor Currency Pairs

- **Exotic and Cross-Currency Pairs:** Due to lower liquidity, consider adjusting RSI parameters and applying additional confirmation tools.

- **Volatility Considerations:** Exotic pairs may exhibit higher volatility, requiring careful risk management and adaptable RSI strategies.

12.3 Cross-Currency Strategies

12.3.1 Identifying Strong and Weak Currencies

- **Comparative RSI Analysis:** Compare RSI levels across multiple currency pairs to identify strength and weakness.

- **Correlation Analysis:** Analyze the correlation between currency pairs to anticipate potential movements in cross-currency pairs.

12.3.2 Carry Trade Considerations

- **Interest Rate Differentials:** Factor in interest rate differentials when considering carry trades. RSI can be used to time entries in the direction of the interest rate advantage.

- **Risk Management:** Carry trades come with inherent risks; use RSI to manage risk by identifying potential reversal points.

Conclusion

Trading currencies with the Relative Strength Index requires a nuanced understanding of Forex market dynamics. Major and minor currency pairs each have distinct characteristics that influence RSI strategy implementation. Cross-currency strategies, considering comparative analysis and interest rate differentials, add an additional layer of complexity. Traders in the Forex market should adapt RSI strategies to suit the unique features of currency trading, combining technical analysis with a deep understanding of global economic factors. As with any trading strategy, ongoing analysis, risk management, and adaptability are key to success in the ever-changing world of Forex markets.

CHAPTER 13

RSI IN CRYPTOCURRENCY TRADING

Cryptocurrency trading introduces a unique set of challenges and opportunities due to the highly volatile nature of digital assets. Integrating the Relative Strength Index (RSI) into cryptocurrency trading strategies requires a tailored approach to navigate the dynamic and often unpredictable crypto markets.

13.1 Volatility in Crypto Markets

13.1.1 Inherent Volatility

- **Market Sentiment Swings:** Cryptocurrencies are highly sensitive to market sentiment, leading to rapid and substantial price fluctuations.

- **24/7 Trading:** Unlike traditional markets, cryptocurrencies trade 24/7, contributing to increased volatility as news and events can impact prices at any time.

13.1.2 External Influences

- **Regulatory Developments:** Regulatory changes or announcements can significantly affect the value of cryptocurrencies.

- **Technological Advancements:** Updates to blockchain technology, security concerns, and innovations in the crypto space can influence market dynamics.

13.2 RSI Strategies for Bitcoin and Altcoins

13.2.1 Bitcoin (BTC) Trading

- **Long-Term Trends:** Use longer RSI periods for assessing Bitcoin's long-term trends. Consider 14 or 21 periods for a broader perspective.

- **Overbought/Oversold Conditions:** Identify potential reversal points during overbought or oversold conditions. Bitcoin often experiences strong trends, and RSI can assist in timing entry and exit points.

13.2.2 Altcoin Trading

- **Altcoin Characteristics:** Altcoins may exhibit different patterns than Bitcoin. Adjust RSI parameters based on the specific characteristics of the altcoin being traded.

- **Volume Analysis:** Incorporate volume analysis with RSI signals to confirm trend strength in altcoins, as liquidity may vary across different tokens.

13.3 ICO and Token Sale Analysis

13.3.1 Assessing ICOs

- **Pre-ICO Analysis:** Use RSI as part of a comprehensive analysis when considering participation in Initial Coin Offerings (ICOs).

Evaluate the project's fundamentals, team, and tokenomics alongside technical indicators.

- **Post-ICO Trading:** Once a token is listed, apply RSI to identify potential entry or exit points. Monitor RSI divergence or convergence for insights into future price movements.

13.3.2 Token Sale Analysis

- **Post-Token Sale Trading:** Apply RSI to tokens that have undergone initial coin offerings or token sales. Use RSI as a tool for timing entry points or managing risk.

- **News and Announcements:** Be mindful of news and announcements that can impact the price of tokens post-sale. RSI can help identify potential market sentiment shifts.

Conclusion

Cryptocurrency trading presents a volatile and ever-evolving landscape. Integrating RSI into trading strategies for Bitcoin, altcoins, ICOs, and token sales requires adaptability and a deep understanding of the unique characteristics of the crypto market. Traders should be vigilant in monitoring market sentiment, news developments, and technological advancements while applying RSI as a valuable tool for technical analysis. As with any asset class, disciplined risk management and continuous learning are key components of success in the cryptocurrency trading space.

CHAPTER 14

RSI STRATEGY FOR OPTIONS TRADING

Options trading introduces a layer of complexity and flexibility to financial markets, allowing traders to hedge, speculate, and implement various strategies. Integrating the Relative Strength Index (RSI) into options trading strategies enhances the precision of timing entries and exits, offering valuable insights for both hedging and speculative purposes.

14.1 Hedging and Speculating with Options

14.1.1 Hedging with Options

- **Protective Puts:** Use options to hedge a long position in a stock by purchasing protective puts. RSI can aid in timing the purchase of puts during overbought conditions or potential trend reversals.

- **Covered Calls:** Write covered calls on existing stock positions to generate income. RSI can assist in identifying suitable entry points for covered call strategies.

14.1.2 Speculating with Options

- **Long Call Options:** Speculate on upward price movements by purchasing call options. RSI signals can help time entries during oversold conditions or potential trend reversals.

- **Long Put Options:** Speculate on downward price movements by purchasing put options. Use RSI to identify entry points during overbought conditions or potential trend reversals.

14.2 RSI as a Tool for Timing Options Trades

14.2.1 Confirming Trends and Reversals

- **Trend Confirmation:** Confirm the strength of a trend before initiating an options trade. RSI above 50 may indicate an uptrend, while RSI below 50 suggests a potential downtrend.

- **Divergence Signals:** Utilize RSI divergence to identify potential trend reversals. Divergence between RSI and price action can be a powerful signal for options traders.

14.2.2 Setting Strike Prices

- **Strike Price Selection:** Use RSI levels to guide the selection of strike prices. In a bullish scenario, consider options with lower strike prices during oversold conditions. In a bearish scenario, focus on higher strike prices during overbought conditions.

- **Dynamic Adjustment:** Adjust strike prices dynamically based on evolving RSI signals to align with changing market conditions.

14.3 Case Studies in Options Trading

14.3.1 Protective Put Strategy

- **Scenario:** An investor holds a significant position in a tech stock anticipating long-term growth.

- **RSI Signal:** RSI reaches overbought levels.

- **Options Strategy:** Purchase protective put options to hedge against potential downside.

14.3.2 Long Call Option Strategy

- **Scenario:** A trader identifies a stock with strong fundamentals and positive RSI divergence.

- **RSI Signal:** RSI shows bullish divergence.

- **Options Strategy:** Execute a long call option to capitalize on the anticipated upward movement.

14.3.3 Covered Call Income Strategy

- **Scenario:** An investor holds a diversified portfolio of blue-chip stocks.

- **RSI Signal:** RSI indicates overbought conditions in the overall market.

- **Options Strategy:** Write covered calls on the existing stock positions to generate income and potentially benefit from stagnant or slightly declining markets.

Conclusion

Integrating RSI into options trading strategies enhances precision and effectiveness, whether for hedging existing positions or speculating on market movements. The dynamic nature of RSI signals provides valuable insights for timing entries and exits in the options market. As with any trading strategy, thorough risk management and adaptability to changing market conditions are crucial for success in options trading. Continuous monitoring of RSI signals and their correlation with options strategies contributes to a well-informed and dynamic approach to navigating the complexities of financial markets.

CHAPTER 15

RSI AND DAY TRADING

Day trading involves executing short-term trades within a single trading day, taking advantage of intraday price movements. The Relative Strength Index (RSI) can be a valuable tool for day traders, providing insights into overbought and oversold conditions, trend strength, and potential reversals. In this chapter, we'll explore intraday strategies with RSI, scalping techniques, and effective risk management for day trading.

15.1 Intraday Strategies with RSI

15.1.1 Intraday Timeframes

- **Selecting RSI Periods:** Adapt RSI periods based on the intraday timeframe. Shorter periods, such as 5 or 10, can provide more responsive signals for intraday trading.

- **Multiple Timeframe Analysis:** Combine RSI signals from different intraday timeframes for a comprehensive view of price dynamics.

15.1.2 Overbought and Oversold Signals

- **Intraday Reversals:** Use RSI to identify potential intraday reversals when the market is overbought or oversold. Enter trades in the opposite direction when RSI signals exhaustion.

- **Trend Confirmation:** Confirm the prevailing intraday trend by assessing RSI levels. In an uptrend, RSI should stay relatively high, while in a downtrend, RSI tends to remain lower.

15.2 Scalping Techniques

15.2.1 Quick Trades with RSI

- **Short-Term Momentum:** RSI can be used to identify short-term momentum shifts for quick scalping opportunities.

- **Low RSI for Long Entries:** Consider long entries when RSI drops into oversold territory, anticipating a potential bounce.

- **High RSI for Short Entries:** Look for short entries when RSI reaches overbought conditions, suggesting a potential retracement.

15.2.2 Tight Stop-Loss and Take-Profit

- **Scalping Dynamics:** Scalpers aim for small price movements, requiring tight risk management.

- **Use of Moving Averages:** Combine RSI with short-term moving averages to confirm trends and set dynamic stop-loss and take-profit levels.

15.3 Managing Risks in Day Trading

15.3.1 Position Sizing

- **Risk Percentage Rule:** Limit each trade's risk to a small percentage of your overall day trading capital.

- **Volatility Adjustment:** Adjust position sizes based on the intraday volatility of the market being traded.

15.3.2 Stop-Loss Orders

- **Dynamic Stops:** Implement dynamic stop-loss orders based on recent price action and RSI signals.

- **Setting Hard Stops:** In fast-moving markets, consider setting hard stops to ensure quick exits in case of adverse price movements.

15.3.3 Diversification and Focus

- **Diversification:** Diversify trades across different instruments or sectors to spread risk.

- **Focused Trades:** Concentrate on a few well-researched opportunities rather than scattering attention across numerous assets.

Conclusion

Day trading with RSI involves adapting traditional strategies to the fast-paced nature of intraday markets. Utilizing RSI for intraday reversals, trend confirmation, and scalping techniques can enhance a day trader's decision-making process. However, effective risk management is paramount in day trading, where markets can change rapidly. Traders should embrace disciplined position sizing, utilize dynamic stop-loss orders, and balance diversification with focused, well-researched trades. The combination of RSI strategies and robust risk management practices can contribute to success in the challenging realm of day trading.

CHAPTER 16

RSI STRATEGY FOR SWING TRADING

Swing trading involves capturing short to medium-term price movements within an established trend. The Relative Strength Index (RSI) serves as a valuable tool for swing traders, providing insights into overbought and oversold conditions, trend strength, and potential reversals. In this chapter, we will explore strategies for swing trading with RSI, setting targets, and implementing effective risk management.

16.1 Holding Positions for Days to Weeks

16.1.1 Swing Trading Timeframes

- **Selecting RSI Periods:** Choose RSI periods that align with the swing trading timeframe. Common choices include 14 or 21 periods for daily charts.

- **Daily and Weekly Charts:** Analyze daily and weekly charts to identify longer-term trends and potential swing trade opportunities.

16.1.2 Trend Identification

- **Distinguishing Trends:** Use RSI to confirm the prevailing trend. In an uptrend, RSI should generally stay above 50, while in a downtrend, RSI tends to remain below 50.

- **Divergence Signals:** Look for divergence between RSI and price action to identify potential trend reversals during swing trading.

16.2 Setting Swing Trading Targets with RSI

16.2.1 RSI Levels for Targets

- **Overbought and Oversold Conditions:** Set swing trade targets based on RSI levels. In an uptrend, consider taking profits when RSI reaches overbought conditions. In a downtrend, look for oversold conditions to cover short positions.

- **Fibonacci Retracement Levels:** Combine RSI with Fibonacci retracement levels to identify potential price targets for swing trades.

16.2.2 Dynamic Target Adjustments

- **Trailing Stop-Loss:** Implement a trailing stop-loss mechanism based on RSI and recent price action. Adjust targets dynamically as the trend progresses.

- **Moving Averages:** Use moving averages alongside RSI to set dynamic targets. Targets can be adjusted based on the interaction between price and moving averages.

16.3 Swing Trading Risk Management

16.3.1 Position Sizing

- **Risk-Per-Trade Percentage:** Limit the risk of each swing trade to a small percentage of your overall swing trading capital.

- **Volatility Considerations:** Adjust position sizes based on the volatility of the market being traded to accommodate varying risk levels.

16.3.2 Stop-Loss Orders

- **Support and Resistance Levels:** Set stop-loss orders based on key support and resistance levels identified through technical analysis.

- **RSI Confirmation:** Use RSI confirmation to place stop-loss orders, ensuring they align with potential trend reversals.

16.3.3 Diversification and Sector Analysis

- **Diversification:** Diversify swing trades across different sectors or industries to spread risk.

- **Sector Strength:** Analyze the strength of sectors using RSI to focus on those with the most favorable trends and potential for swing trade opportunities.

Conclusion

Swing trading with RSI provides a systematic approach to capturing short to medium-term price movements. By adapting RSI to the swing trading timeframe, identifying trends, and setting dynamic targets with effective risk management, traders can increase the probability of successful swing trades. Remember, consistent profitability in swing trading involves a combination of technical analysis, risk management, and adaptability to changing market conditions. As you apply RSI strategies to your swing trading approach, remain disciplined and continuously refine your methodology for ongoing success.

CHAPTER 17

RSI STRATEGY FOR LONG-TERM INVESTORS

Long-term investing requires a strategic approach to building and managing a portfolio over an extended period. The Relative Strength Index (RSI) can be a valuable tool for long-term investors, providing insights into trends, potential reversals, and opportunities for optimizing asset allocation. In this chapter, we'll explore strategies for long-term investors using RSI in portfolio management, timing long-term investments, and making informed decisions about asset allocation.

17.1 RSI in Portfolio Management

17.1.1 Portfolio Diversification

- **Diversification Benefits:** Utilize RSI to assess the strength of individual assets within a diversified portfolio. RSI signals can complement other fundamental and technical analyses.

- **Correlation Analysis:** Combine RSI with correlation analysis to understand how assets in the portfolio interact and identify potential rebalancing opportunities.

17.1.2 Volatility Management

- **Volatility Assessment:** RSI can assist in assessing the volatility of individual assets. Lower RSI levels may indicate lower volatility, while higher RSI levels may suggest increased market activity.

- **Risk Mitigation:** Adjust portfolio weightings based on RSI signals to mitigate risk during periods of heightened volatility.

17.2 Using RSI to Time Long-Term Investments

17.2.1 Trend Confirmation

- **Confirming Long-Term Trends:** RSI can confirm the strength of long-term trends. In an uptrend, RSI should generally stay above 50, while in a downtrend, RSI tends to remain below 50.

- **Divergence Signals:** Utilize RSI divergence to identify potential reversals or shifts in long-term trends. Divergence between RSI and price action can be a powerful signal for long-term investors.

17.2.2 Dynamic Entry Points

- **Market Timing:** Use RSI to time entry points for long-term investments. Enter positions when RSI signals oversold conditions in an uptrend or overbought conditions in a downtrend.

- **Combining RSI with Fundamental Analysis:** Integrate RSI with fundamental analysis to enhance the timing of long-term investments. Confirm RSI signals with strong fundamentals for more robust decision-making.

17.3 Asset Allocation and RSI Signals

17.3.1 Allocating Capital

- **RSI-Based Capital Allocation:** Allocate capital to different assets based on their RSI signals. Favor assets with lower RSI levels for potential long-term entries and consider reducing exposure to those with higher RSI levels.

- **Sector Rotation:** Use RSI to assess the strength of various sectors. Rotate capital into sectors showing relative strength and allocate away from weaker sectors.

17.3.2 Rebalancing Strategies

- **Periodic Rebalancing:** Incorporate RSI signals into periodic portfolio rebalancing. Adjust allocations based on changing market conditions to maintain the desired risk-return profile.

- **Dynamic Asset Allocation:** Dynamically adjust asset allocation using RSI signals to capitalize on changing market trends and economic conditions.

Conclusion

Long-term investing with RSI involves combining the benefits of technical analysis with a strategic, patient approach to portfolio management. By integrating RSI into portfolio decisions, long-term investors can enhance their ability to identify trends, time entries and exits, and optimize asset allocation. Remember, successful long-term investing requires a disciplined adherence to a well-defined investment strategy, considering both technical and fundamental factors. As you apply RSI strategies to your long-term investment approach, focus on the broader goals of wealth preservation and growth over time.

CHAPTER 18

AUTOMATION AND RSI TRADING BOTS

Automated trading systems, powered by algorithms and artificial intelligence, have gained popularity in financial markets. The Relative Strength Index (RSI), a widely used technical indicator, can be incorporated into trading bots for systematic and algorithmic trading. In this chapter, we will explore building RSI trading algorithms, discuss the pros and cons of automated RSI trading, and examine future trends in algorithmic RSI trading.

18.1 Building RSI Trading Algorithms

18.1.1 Algorithm Development

- **Programming Languages:** Use languages like Python, R, or C++ to code trading algorithms that incorporate RSI signals.

- **API Integration:** Connect algorithms to financial market APIs for real-time data feeds, enabling dynamic decision-making.

18.1.2 RSI Signal Integration

- **RSI Parameters:** Define RSI periods and overbought/oversold thresholds based on the strategy's objectives and historical analysis.

- **Signal Confirmation:** Combine RSI signals with other technical indicators or price action patterns for enhanced accuracy.

18.1.3 Backtesting and Optimization

- **Historical Data Analysis:** Backtest algorithms using historical data to assess performance and optimize RSI parameters.

- **Risk Management:** Implement risk management features within the algorithm, such as stop-loss and take-profit mechanisms.

18.2 Pros and Cons of Automated RSI Trading

18.2.1 Pros

- **Emotionless Execution:** Automated systems execute trades without emotional biases, ensuring adherence to predefined strategies.

- **Speed and Efficiency:** Trading bots operate at high speeds, enabling quick responses to market changes and opportunities.

- **24/7 Availability:** Bots can monitor markets and execute trades around the clock, taking advantage of global trading opportunities.

18.2.2 Cons

- **Technical Risks:** System glitches, connectivity issues, or bugs in the algorithm can lead to unexpected outcomes and losses.

- **Market Dynamics:** Rapid market changes or unforeseen events may challenge the adaptability of automated systems.

- **Over-Optimization:** Excessive fine-tuning based on historical data (over-optimization) may lead to poor performance in live markets.

18.3 Future Trends in Algorithmic RSI Trading

18.3.1 Machine Learning Integration

- **Adaptive Algorithms:** Incorporate machine learning techniques to enable algorithms to adapt to changing market conditions.

- **Pattern Recognition:** Train algorithms to recognize evolving market patterns and optimize strategies accordingly.

18.3.2 Sentiment Analysis

- **Social Media and News Integration:** Integrate sentiment analysis tools to gauge market sentiment and adjust trading strategies accordingly.

- **News-Based Trading:** Develop algorithms that respond to breaking news and events, incorporating sentiment data.

18.3.3 Regulatory Compliance

- **Compliance Algorithms:** Design algorithms that adhere to evolving financial regulations and compliance standards.

- **Risk Management Enhancements:** Implement features that enhance risk management and comply with regulatory requirements.

Conclusion

Automated RSI trading brings efficiency and objectivity to the execution of trading strategies. Building algorithms that integrate RSI signals requires a thoughtful approach to programming, signal integration, and risk management. While automated trading offers numerous advantages, it's crucial to recognize and manage potential risks. Future trends in algorithmic RSI trading involve the integration of machine learning, sentiment analysis, and a focus on regulatory compliance. As technology continues to advance, traders and developers should stay attuned to these trends to harness the full potential of automated RSI trading in evolving financial landscapes.

CHAPTER 19

RSI AND ECONOMIC INDICATORS

The Relative Strength Index (RSI), a popular technical indicator, is typically associated with individual securities or markets. However, its application extends beyond charts and price movements. In this chapter, we explore how RSI can be used as a tool to gauge economic trends, analyze macro-economic data, and provide insights into global economic perspectives.

19.1 RSI as an Economic Trend Indicator

19.1.1 Economic Cycle Alignment

- **Business Cycle Phases:** Align RSI signals with different phases of the economic cycle, such as expansion, contraction, peak, and trough.

- **Leading Indicator:** RSI can act as a leading indicator, providing early signals of potential shifts in economic trends.

19.1.2 Unemployment and RSI

- **Correlation Analysis:** Explore the correlation between RSI levels and unemployment rates. RSI signals may precede changes in employment trends.

- **Labor Market Health:** Use RSI to assess the health of the labor market, identifying potential turning points.

19.2 Analyzing Macro-Economic Data with RSI

19.2.1 GDP Growth and RSI

- **Correlation with GDP:** Examine the correlation between RSI levels and Gross Domestic Product (GDP) growth rates. RSI signals may precede changes in economic output.

- **Investment Timing:** Utilize RSI to time investments based on expectations of economic growth or contraction.

19.2.2 Interest Rates and RSI

- **Central Bank Policy:** Align RSI signals with central bank policy changes. RSI can provide insights into potential shifts in interest rate directions.

- **Debt Management:** Use RSI to assess the impact of interest rate changes on debt management and financial markets.

19.3 Global Economic Perspectives

19.3.1 Currency Strength and RSI

- **Currency Analysis:** Apply RSI to analyze the strength of different currencies. Identify potential shifts in global economic perspectives based on currency movements.

- **Trade Balances:** Use RSI to assess trade balances and potential impacts on global economic perspectives.

19.3.2 Commodity Prices and RSI

- **Commodity Markets:** Apply RSI to commodity prices to gain insights into global economic trends. Commodity movements can reflect shifts in demand and supply dynamics.

- **Inflation Expectations:** Monitor RSI signals in commodity markets to gauge inflation expectations and potential economic implications.

Conclusion

Using RSI as an economic indicator provides a unique perspective on economic trends, complementing traditional economic indicators. Whether analyzing unemployment rates, GDP growth, interest rates, or global economic factors, RSI can offer valuable insights. As economic landscapes evolve, traders, analysts, and policymakers can incorporate RSI into their toolkit for a more comprehensive understanding of economic dynamics. While RSI is not a standalone economic indicator, its integration with macro-economic data can contribute to a more nuanced and timely interpretation of economic trends at both the national and global levels.

CHAPTER 20

RSI IN A TECHNOLOGICAL WORLD

The evolution of technology has transformed financial markets, introducing new opportunities and challenges. The Relative Strength Index (RSI), a traditional technical indicator, has adapted to the demands of the technological world. In this chapter, we explore the utilization of RSI in high-frequency trading, the integration of artificial intelligence with RSI, and the applications of RSI in the context of blockchain technology.

20.1 Utilizing RSI in High-Frequency Trading

20.1.1 Speed and Precision

- **Intraday Trading Dynamics:** Leverage RSI for rapid decision-making in high-frequency trading environments.

- **Adaptive RSI Parameters:** Adjust RSI periods dynamically to align with the fast-paced nature of high-frequency markets.

20.1.2 Algorithmic Execution

- **Automated Trading Strategies:** Implement algorithms that use RSI signals to execute trades swiftly and efficiently.

- **Latency Considerations:** Optimize algorithms for low-latency execution to capitalize on short-term price movements identified by RSI.

20.2 Artificial Intelligence and RSI

20.2.1 Machine Learning Integration

- **Predictive Analytics:** Combine RSI with machine learning algorithms to enhance the predictive power of trading models.

- **Pattern Recognition:** Train AI models to recognize complex patterns in RSI data, providing more nuanced trading signals.

20.2.2 Algorithmic Decision-Making

- **Dynamic Strategy Optimization:** Employ artificial intelligence to continuously optimize trading strategies based on evolving RSI signals and market conditions.

- **Risk Management:** Integrate AI-based risk management tools that adapt to changing market dynamics identified by RSI.

20.3 Blockchain and RSI Applications

20.3.1 Smart Contracts and RSI

- **Automated Trading on the Blockchain:** Utilize smart contracts on blockchain platforms for automated trading based on RSI signals.

- **Transparency and Security:** Leverage blockchain's transparency and security features to enhance the reliability of RSI-driven trading systems.

20.3.2 Tokenized Assets and RSI

- **Tokenized Securities:** Apply RSI strategies to tokenized assets, optimizing trading decisions in the evolving landscape of digital securities.

- **Decentralized Exchanges:** Explore RSI-based trading strategies within decentralized exchanges powered by blockchain technology.

Conclusion

In a world driven by technology, RSI continues to be a versatile tool for traders and investors. The adoption of RSI in high-frequency trading environments emphasizes its adaptability to fast-paced markets. Integrating artificial intelligence with RSI enhances predictive capabilities and algorithmic decision-making. In the realm of blockchain, RSI finds applications in automated trading through smart contracts and the optimization of strategies for tokenized assets. As technology continues to advance, the synergy between RSI and emerging technologies will likely lead to innovative approaches in trading and investment strategies. Traders and developers should remain agile, exploring new possibilities and refining RSI applications in response to the evolving technological landscape.

CHAPTER 21

RISK MANAGEMENT STRATEGIES

Effective risk management is paramount to long-term success in trading and investing. The Relative Strength Index (RSI) can play a crucial role in implementing sound risk management strategies. In this chapter, we explore position sizing with RSI, setting stop-loss orders, and portfolio diversification techniques to manage risks in various market scenarios.

21.1 Position Sizing with RSI

21.1.1 Determining Position Size

- **Risk-Per-Trade Percentage:** Define a percentage of your total trading capital that you are willing to risk on a single trade.

- **Volatility Adjustment:** Adjust position sizes based on the volatility of the market being traded. Higher volatility may warrant smaller positions to accommodate potential price swings.

21.1.2 RSI Confirmation for Position Sizing

- **Overbought/Oversold Levels:** Use RSI signals to confirm position sizing decisions. Consider smaller positions in overbought or oversold conditions where the potential for a reversal may be higher.

- **Divergence Analysis:** Factor in RSI divergence or convergence signals when determining the size of a position. Divergence may indicate a weakening trend, influencing position size.

21.2 Setting Stop-Loss Orders

21.2.1 Dynamic Stop-Loss Placement

- **Recent Price Action:** Use recent price action alongside RSI signals to dynamically place stop-loss orders.

- **Volatility Considerations:** Adjust stop-loss levels based on market volatility. Higher volatility may require wider stop-loss orders.

21.2.2 RSI Confirmation for Stop-Loss

- **Confirmation of Trend Reversals:** Utilize RSI to confirm potential trend reversals and adjust stop-loss orders accordingly.

- **Support and Resistance Levels:** Align stop-loss levels with key support and resistance levels identified through technical analysis, ensuring they coincide with RSI signals.

21.3 Portfolio Diversification with RSI

21.3.1 Asset Allocation Based on RSI Signals

- **Capital Allocation:** Allocate capital to assets based on their RSI signals. Favor assets with lower RSI levels for potential entries and consider reducing exposure to those with higher RSI levels.

- **Sector Rotation:** Utilize RSI to assess the strength of various sectors. Rotate capital into sectors showing relative strength and allocate away from weaker sectors.

21.3.2 RSI and Market Correlation

- **Correlation Analysis:** Assess the correlation between RSI signals of different assets in a portfolio. Diversify across assets with less correlated RSI movements to spread risk.

- **Risk Mitigation:** Use RSI as a tool to manage overall portfolio risk by diversifying across assets with diverse RSI dynamics.

Conclusion

Risk management is an integral aspect of successful trading and investing. Position sizing with RSI ensures that the size of each trade aligns with the trader's risk tolerance and market conditions. Setting stop-loss orders based on RSI signals helps protect capital and manage downside risk. Portfolio diversification with RSI adds an additional layer of risk mitigation by allocating capital across assets and sectors based on their respective RSI dynamics. As traders and investors integrate RSI into their risk management strategies, they create a more robust framework for navigating the uncertainties of financial markets while aiming for long-term success.

CHAPTER 22

RSI PITFALLS AND COMMON MISTAKES

While the Relative Strength Index (RSI) is a powerful tool, traders and investors must be mindful of potential pitfalls and common mistakes that can undermine its effectiveness. In this chapter, we explore three key areas—overlooking market context, chasing losses, and avoiding common traps—to help practitioners navigate the nuances of RSI trading.

22.1 Overlooking Market Context

22.1.1 Importance of Market Context

- **Understanding Market Conditions:** RSI signals should be interpreted in the broader context of market conditions. A high RSI in a strong uptrend may not necessarily indicate overbought conditions.

- **Trend Confirmation:** RSI signals are more reliable when they align with the prevailing market trend. Overlooking the context of the trend can lead to misinterpretation.

22.1.2 Adapting to Different Timeframes

- **Timeframe Considerations:** RSI signals can vary based on the timeframe being analyzed. Traders should adapt their strategies and interpretations accordingly.

- **Combining Timeframes:** Utilize multiple timeframes to confirm RSI signals and gain a more comprehensive understanding of market dynamics.

22.2 Chasing Losses

22.2.1 Emotional Decision-Making

- **Revenge Trading:** Chasing losses after a failed trade can lead to impulsive decision-making. Emotional responses can cloud judgment and contribute to further losses.

- **Discipline and Patience:** Adhere to a disciplined trading plan and exercise patience. Accepting losses as part of the trading process is crucial for long-term success.

22.2.2 Risk Management

- **Position Sizing:** Avoid excessively large position sizes in an attempt to recover losses quickly. Maintain consistent risk-per-trade percentages to manage potential drawdowns.

- **Stop-Loss Orders:** Set and adhere to predetermined stop-loss levels. Chasing losses often involves neglecting risk management principles, leading to increased exposure.

22.3 Avoiding Common Traps in RSI Trading

22.3.1 Relying Solely on RSI

- **Confirmation with Other Indicators:** RSI should not be the sole determinant for trading decisions. Confirm signals with other technical indicators, price action, or fundamental analysis.

- **Divergence Signals:** While divergence is a powerful signal, not all divergences result in trend reversals. Consider additional factors before relying solely on divergence.

22.3.2 Ignoring Overbought and Oversold Conditions

- **Trend Strength:** Overbought conditions in a strong uptrend may persist, and oversold conditions in a strong downtrend may also continue. RSI signals should be interpreted in the broader trend context.

- **Contrarian Approach:** Exercise caution when adopting a contrarian approach solely based on overbought or oversold RSI levels. Trend confirmation is crucial.

Conclusion

Successfully navigating RSI trading requires an awareness of potential pitfalls and the discipline to avoid common mistakes. Overlooking market context, chasing losses, and relying solely on RSI are pitfalls that can impact trading outcomes. Traders and investors should prioritize a holistic approach, considering market conditions, emotional discipline, and risk management principles. By acknowledging these pitfalls and learning from common mistakes, practitioners can refine their RSI strategies, enhancing their ability to make informed decisions in the dynamic landscape of financial markets.

CHAPTER 23

REVIEWING REAL-WORLD RSI TRADING SCENARIOS

Learning from real-world trading scenarios provides valuable insights into the practical application of Relative Strength Index (RSI) strategies. In this chapter, we delve into case studies of successful RSI trades, the importance of learning from trading mistakes, and the necessity of adapting strategies to evolving markets.

23.1 Case Studies of Successful RSI Trades

23.1.1 Identifying Trend Reversals

- **Uptrend Reversal:** A case study where RSI correctly identified an overbought condition in a strong uptrend, signaling an impending reversal. Traders used this signal to exit long positions or initiate short positions, resulting in profitable outcomes.

- **Downtrend Reversal:** Examining a scenario where RSI detected oversold conditions during a persistent downtrend, indicating a potential reversal. Traders who recognized this signal might have entered long positions, capitalizing on the subsequent trend shift.

23.1.2 Divergence Signals

- **Bullish Divergence:** Analyzing a successful trade where RSI exhibited bullish divergence with price action. Traders who recognized this pattern might have anticipated a trend reversal, resulting in profitable trades.

- **Bearish Divergence:** Exploring a case where RSI displayed bearish divergence, warning of potential weakness in an ongoing uptrend. Traders leveraging this signal could have adjusted their positions accordingly, avoiding losses in the subsequent correction.

23.2 Learning from Trading Mistakes

23.2.1 Ignoring Market Context

- **Case of Overlooking Context:** Reviewing a trade where RSI signals were misinterpreted due to neglecting broader market context. This scenario emphasizes the importance of considering the overall trend and market conditions.

- **Adapting to Different Timeframes:** Learning from a mistake related to disregarding the impact of different timeframes on RSI signals. Traders should adapt their strategies to align with the chosen timeframe for analysis.

23.2.2 Emotional Decision-Making

- **Revenge Trading Example:** Examining a scenario where emotional responses led to chasing losses after a failed RSI trade. Traders can learn from this mistake by focusing on disciplined, rational decision-making.

- **Discipline and Patience:** Learning from instances where impatience and emotional decision-making resulted in missed opportunities or premature exits. Emphasizing the importance of discipline and patience in adhering to the trading plan.

23.3 Adapting Strategies to Evolving Markets

23.3.1 Integrating New Information

- **Market News and RSI:** Discussing scenarios where unexpected market news influenced RSI signals. Traders need to adapt to changing information and consider both technical and fundamental factors.

- **Evolving Economic Conditions:** Analyzing the impact of evolving economic conditions on RSI strategies. Traders should regularly reassess their approach based on the changing economic landscape.

23.3.2 Cryptocurrency Market Dynamics

- **Volatility in Cryptocurrencies:** Examining the unique challenges and opportunities presented by the highly volatile cryptocurrency markets. RSI strategies need to be tailored to the specific dynamics of digital assets.

- **Incorporating Regulatory Developments:** Adapting strategies in response to regulatory developments affecting the cryptocurrency space. Traders must stay informed and adjust their approaches accordingly.

Conclusion

Reviewing real-world RSI trading scenarios provides a practical understanding of the indicator's effectiveness and challenges. Case studies of successful trades highlight the potential of RSI strategies, while analyzing mistakes underscores the importance of emotional discipline and risk management. Adapting strategies to evolving markets emphasizes the dynamic nature of trading, requiring continuous learning and adjustment. Traders who actively engage with real-world scenarios, learning from both successes and mistakes, are better equipped to refine their RSI strategies and navigate the complexities of financial markets.

CHAPTER 24

FUTURE DEVELOPMENTS IN RSI TRADING

As financial markets continue to evolve, the role of the Relative Strength Index (RSI) in trading strategies is also likely to undergo transformations. In this chapter, we explore potential future developments in RSI trading, considering the impact of emerging technologies, evolving market dynamics, and the necessity of adapting strategies for the future.

24.1 Emerging Technologies and RSI

24.1.1 Artificial Intelligence Integration

- **Advanced Predictive Models:** Future RSI trading strategies may incorporate more advanced predictive models driven by artificial intelligence. Machine learning algorithms could enhance the ability to forecast market trends and RSI signals.

- **Automated Decision-Making:** Integration with AI may lead to more sophisticated automated trading systems that dynamically adapt to changing market conditions, providing traders with real-time insights and execution capabilities.

24.1.2 Blockchain and Decentralized Trading

- **Smart Contracts for RSI-Based Trades:** The use of blockchain and smart contracts may facilitate decentralized RSI-based trading. Traders could execute automated, trustless trades based on RSI signals directly on blockchain platforms.

- **Tokenized Assets and RSI Strategies:** As more assets become tokenized, RSI strategies may be adapted to the tokenized environment. Traders might develop strategies specific to digital assets, considering the unique characteristics of tokenized securities.

24.2 Evolving Market Dynamics

24.2.1 Global Market Connectivity

- **Interconnected Global Markets:** RSI strategies may evolve to consider the interconnectedness of global markets. Traders might incorporate RSI signals from various markets to gain a more comprehensive understanding of trends.

- **Real-Time Data Integration:** With advancements in technology, RSI strategies could leverage real-time data integration across different asset classes, allowing for more accurate and timely decision-making.

24.2.2 Regulatory Developments

- **Compliance in Algorithmic Trading:** Future RSI strategies may place greater emphasis on compliance with evolving regulatory standards. Traders might need to adapt algorithms to meet the requirements of regulatory authorities.

- **Impact of Regulatory Changes on RSI Signals:** Changes in financial regulations may influence market dynamics and subsequently impact RSI signals. Traders will need to stay informed about regulatory developments and adjust strategies accordingly.

24.3 Adapting Strategies for the Future

24.3.1 Continuous Learning and Research

- **Staying Informed:** Future traders using RSI strategies should prioritize continuous learning and stay informed about advancements in technical analysis, market dynamics, and emerging technologies.

- **Research and Development:** A commitment to research and development will be crucial. Traders may need to explore new indicators, refine existing models, and test strategies in evolving market conditions.

24.3.2 Flexibility and Adaptability

- **Dynamic Strategy Adjustment:** Future RSI strategies must be flexible and adaptable to changing market environments. Traders should develop mechanisms for dynamically adjusting parameters and rules based on current conditions.

- **Scenario Analysis:** Traders may engage in scenario analysis, preparing for various market scenarios and tailoring RSI strategies to address different economic conditions and geopolitical events.

Conclusion

The future of RSI trading holds exciting possibilities as technology continues to advance, markets evolve, and regulatory landscapes shift. Traders who embrace emerging technologies like artificial intelligence and blockchain, understand evolving market dynamics, and continuously adapt their strategies will be well-positioned for success. Staying informed, conducting ongoing research, and maintaining flexibility in approach are key principles for traders looking to navigate the dynamic future of RSI trading. As the landscape unfolds, the synergy between innovation and tried-and-true technical analysis principles will shape the next generation of RSI strategies.

CHAPTER 25

THE ROAD TO MASTERY

Becoming a master in RSI trading requires a commitment to continual learning, the development of a personalized trading system, and a dedication to honing your skills over time. In this chapter, we explore the essential elements of the road to mastery in RSI trading.

25.1 Continual Learning and Improvement

25.1.1 Staying Informed

- **Market Updates:** Regularly stay informed about market news, economic events, and global trends. Understanding the broader financial landscape enhances your ability to interpret RSI signals effectively.

- **Technical Analysis Advances:** Keep abreast of advancements in technical analysis. Attend workshops, webinars, and engage with trading communities to learn about new indicators, strategies, and market insights.

25.1.2 Analyzing Trading Results

- **Performance Evaluation:** Regularly evaluate your trading performance. Analyze successful trades to understand what worked well and learn from losses to identify areas for improvement.

- **Journaling Trades:** Maintain a trading journal to document your decisions, emotional states, and the rationale behind each trade. Reflecting on past trades enhances self-awareness and aids in refining your approach.

25.2 Building a Personalized RSI Trading System

25.2.1 Defining Your Trading Goals

- **Setting Objectives:** Clearly define your trading goals, whether they are focused on short-term gains, long-term wealth accumulation, or a specific risk-return profile. Your trading system should align with these objectives.

- **Risk Tolerance:** Understand and establish your risk tolerance. A personalized trading system should incorporate risk management strategies that align with your comfort level.

25.2.2 Developing a Trading Plan

- **Entry and Exit Rules:** Clearly outline your entry and exit rules based on RSI signals and other indicators. Having predefined rules reduces emotional decision-making and fosters consistency in your trading.

- **Risk Management Strategies:** Integrate risk management strategies into your plan, including position sizing, stop-loss orders, and portfolio diversification based on RSI dynamics.

25.3 Becoming a Master RSI Trader

25.3.1 Practice and Experience

- **Backtesting:** Conduct thorough backtesting of your trading system using historical data. This practice helps refine your strategy, identify weaknesses, and gain confidence in your approach.

- **Simulated Trading:** Utilize simulated trading platforms to practice your strategy in real-time market conditions without risking capital. This allows you to refine your execution skills and adapt to dynamic markets.

25.3.2 Adaptability and Continuous Improvement

- **Adapting to Market Changes:** Stay adaptable to changing market conditions. Periodically reassess and adjust your trading system to remain effective in evolving financial landscapes.

- **Continuous Learning:** Embrace a mindset of continuous learning. Engage with the trading community, read relevant literature, and attend seminars to stay abreast of new developments in RSI trading and financial markets.

25.3.3 Emotional Discipline

- **Mastering Emotions:** Emotional discipline is a hallmark of a master trader. Develop strategies to manage emotions such as fear and greed, and maintain a rational mindset even during challenging market conditions.

- **Learning from Mistakes:** View mistakes as opportunities for learning and improvement. A master RSI trader acknowledges and learns from errors, continually refining their approach.

Conclusion

The road to mastery in RSI trading is a journey that combines knowledge, experience, and a commitment to personal growth. Continual learning, the development of a personalized trading system, and the cultivation of emotional discipline are essential elements of this journey. Becoming a master RSI trader requires adaptability, resilience, and a dedication to continuous improvement. As you progress along this road, embrace challenges as opportunities, learn from both successes and mistakes, and refine your skills to navigate the dynamic landscape of financial markets with confidence and expertise.

APPENDIX

RSI TRADING EXERCISES

The following exercises are designed to help traders practice using the Relative Strength Index (RSI) indicator in various market scenarios. These exercises aim to enhance your understanding of RSI signals, improve decision-making skills, and reinforce the application of RSI strategies.

Exercise 1: Trend Reversal Identification

Objective: Identify potential trend reversals using RSI signals.

1. Select a financial instrument or asset class with historical price data.

2. Examine instances where RSI indicated overbought or oversold conditions.

3. Identify subsequent price movements and confirm if trend reversals occurred.

4. Document your observations and insights in a trading journal.

Exercise 2: Divergence Analysis

Objective: Recognize bullish and bearish divergence signals.

1. Choose a trading pair or asset with sufficient historical data.

2. Locate instances where price movements diverge from RSI trends.

3. Analyze the impact of bullish divergence on subsequent price action.

4. Investigate how bearish divergence aligns with trend reversals.

5. Document your findings and consider potential trading strategies based on divergence signals.

Exercise 3: Dynamic Position Sizing

Objective: Practice dynamic position sizing based on RSI signals.

1. Select a financial instrument or asset.

2. Develop a strategy that dynamically adjusts position sizes based on RSI levels.

3. Implement your strategy on historical data, considering various RSI thresholds.

4. Assess the impact of dynamic position sizing on overall portfolio performance.

5. Refine your position sizing strategy based on the exercise outcomes.

Exercise 4: Setting Adaptive Stop-Loss Orders

Objective: Practice setting stop-loss orders based on evolving RSI signals.

1. Choose a trading pair or asset.

2. Develop a strategy that adapts stop-loss levels according to RSI dynamics.

3. Simulate trading scenarios where RSI signals change over time.

4. Evaluate the effectiveness of adaptive stop-loss orders in minimizing losses.

5. Adjust your strategy based on the exercise results.

Exercise 5: Scenario-Based Trading

Objective: Apply RSI strategies in different market scenarios.

1. Select multiple financial instruments representing diverse market conditions.

2. Develop RSI strategies tailored to bullish, bearish, and sideways markets.

3. Simulate trades in various scenarios, considering economic events and news.

4. Assess the performance of RSI strategies under different market conditions.

5. Identify commonalities and differences in strategy effectiveness.

Exercise 6: Real-Time Trading Simulation

Objective: Simulate real-time trading using RSI signals.

1. Choose a live market or use historical data for a recent period.

2. Simulate trades based on real-time RSI signals, without actual capital at risk.

3. Record your decisions, entry/exit points, and observations.

4. Assess the accuracy of RSI signals and the effectiveness of your trading decisions.

5. Reflect on the experience to refine your approach.

Remember to approach these exercises with a mindset of continuous learning. Regularly review your performance, adapt your strategies, and refine your understanding of RSI dynamics. Trading exercises can significantly contribute to your skill development and overall proficiency as an RSI trader.

www.ingramcontent.com/pod-product-compliance
Lightning Source LLC
Chambersburg PA
CBHW072255310526
45795CB00012B/1457